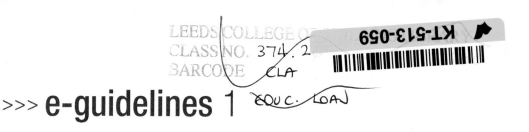

>>> **e-guidelines** 1

Online resources in the classroom

Using the World Wide Web to deliver
and support adult learning

Alan Clarke and Claudia Hesse

niace

promoting adult learning

©2004 National Institute of Adult Continuing Education
(England and Wales)
21 De Montfort Street
Leicester
LE1 7GE

Company registration no. 2603322
Charity registration no. 1002775

NIACE has a broad remit to promote lifelong learning opportunities for adults. NIACE works to develop increased participation in education and training, particularly for those who do not have easy access because of class, gender, age, race, language and culture, learning difficulties or disabilities, or insufficient financial resources.

You can find NIACE online at www.niace.org.uk

Cataloguing in Publication Data
A CIP record of this title is available from the British Library

Designed and typeset by Patrick Armstrong Book Production Services, London

Printed and bound in the UK by Latimer Trend
ISBN: 1 86201 224 5

Contents

Photo: Nick Hayes

Acknowledgements

We would like to acknowledge support from the National Learning
Network and Prudential plc in developing this guide. Also we would
like to acknowledge the support of the Wolverhampton Adult
Education Service, the Brasshouse Language Centre in Birmingham,
Bromley Adult Education College, and Age Concern, Chislehurst, who
kindly let us take photographs with their learners at their premises.

Photo: Nick Hayes

1

About this guide

Introduction

This is a practical guide on how to use the resources available on the World Wide Web to deliver and support learning. It is intended to help tutors of any subject, but we have also developed a specific on-line guide to using the resources available within the 'Money matters to me' website, which is focused on financial education. You may find it beneficial to visit the site and consider the specific guide (**www.moneymatterstome.co.uk**). *This* guide will use 'Money matters to me' as an example to illustrate ideas and concepts.

Who is this guide for?

This book is designed for tutors of any subject who are seeking to use the vast resources of the Web in their teaching – that is, using online resources in a face-to-face context. It assumes that you will be integrating the resources into your teaching and learning activities. This process is called blended learning, and is widely seen as an effective way of gaining the benefits of both traditional and e-learning approaches.

What is the aim of this guide?

It will help you to use online resources in a variety of ways to aid learning, such as developing online exercises and activities such as Webquests, worksheets, quizzes, investigations, and creating online content. Also, it gives you a glossary of the most important terms.

What will you find in this guide?

It will provide you with advice based on existing practice.

2

Learning

The Web has enormous potential to aid learning. However, realising that potential does require an understanding of learning, the Web and online approaches.

Some fundamentals

Learning is an active process. If you observe someone using the Web it quickly becomes clear that it, too, is an active process. Users are continuously required to make choices – what links to go to, whether to scroll down the page, jump back to an earlier page, bookmark or print this page or another. Users have to make these decisions while trying to read, although often by browsing or scanning the content to identify what they are seeking.

Many adults find using the Web an engaging and enjoyable process. However, for some new users the Web is also frightening and intimidating in that it is huge and different from their previous experiences. Before adults can benefit from learning through the Web they do need to be confident that they can use it. Later we will consider some ways of using the Web to develop learners' confidence and competence in using it.

The benefits of e-learning

When you are planning the use of online resources to enhance the learning experience you should be aware of the potential benefits of e-learning; that is, when e-learning is likely to add most value to your courses. Some of the main reported benefits are:

> Many adults are interested in learning to use ICT, so they will be
>   *motivated* if it forms part of a course.

> Technology can sometimes provide new or alternative ways of presenting information so that you can *meet the different learning-style preferences of your learners.*

> Using e-learning in your teaching can *support active learning.*

> Learning with the support of ICT offers the additional advantage of *gaining ICT skills and knowledge.*

> Online learning can give learners *more choice about where, when and how quickly they learn.* It is important to build on this potential when you are designing learning experiences.

> Adults who have had *previously poor experiences* of education often do not associate ICT with these negative experiences, so they are more likely to be willing to participate.

The purpose of e-learning

To gain the benefits of access to the Web requires purpose. Learners need to have a reason for searching and browsing. If they have clear objectives and an understanding of what they are doing they will gain the maximum benefits. Without clear aims, it can become the equivalent of skimming through a newspaper or browsing in a bookshop, so if they benefit from the experience it will be owing to chance.

A key factor in using online resources successfully is to consider the learning objectives and what the learners will be able to do or understand after the experience. This is good practice in all contexts.

The tutor's role

Integrating online resources into learning tends to assume a learner-centred approach. In this guide we focus on examples that follow this approach and that demonstrate the use of the Web to enhance the learning process. Our focus is on what is most beneficial for the learners, not on the resources themselves. The scope of information and other resources available across the Web allows you to provide a context that is meaningful to the individual learner. This is a powerful motivator, but it does influence the role of the tutor in that it is unlikely that you will be an expert on every subject which interests your learners. The role is therefore more that of facilitator and supporter of learning rather than a source of knowledge.

Example

The 'Money matters to me' website offers a structure based on an individual's life changes (Figure 1). If a whole class were using the resource, then potentially they could all be exploring different financial issues. Using the 'Life changes' section would allow learners to choose content that is relevant to their lives, which would be a meaningful and motivating experience for them. Your role as tutor would be to support your learners, not control what they are learning – at times you may want to direct them to consider a particular piece of content, but often this is the result of one learner locating it and you realising its relevance to the whole group.

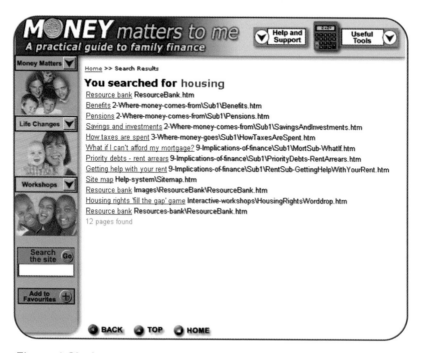

Figure 1 **Choice www.moneymatterstome.co.uk**

You can adopt several approaches with online materials, depending on your use of them. You might:

> Check all sites before allowing learners to use them, in which case you are following the traditional tutor's role in that you will have more understanding of the content than your learners – this is perfectly sound.
> Use the Web as an enormous resource for investigations, assignments and exercises. With this approach, it is unlikely that you will have seen many of the sites before, so your role is more supporting and facilitative for searching, judging quality and helping learners identify alternative sources of information. This approach can enhance learners' critical and analytical skills. You might find that this approach is more suitable for advanced learners/Internet users.

The choice is largely your own, but it is important to make sure your learners understand your role.

Constructivism

The constructivist approach to learning is widely seen as highly appropriate to e-learning, so you should be aware of its basic features in order to adopt them in your classes. It is based on the view that learners are not passively waiting to be filled with knowledge, but are active partners in the process and come to the class with many life experiences to build on. The tutor's role is not to lecture, but to guide and facilitate learning. The emphasis is on interactive participative learning, with the tutor asking questions, provoking discussion, and encouraging peer support, and group activities.

An important element in constructivist approaches is that learners reflect on what they are experiencing, and are encouraged to bring their previous experiences into the process and construct new understanding for themselves. The tutor assists with questions, encouraging learners to work together in a co-operative and collaborative way. A feature of constructivism is the provision of information, which learners can interpret. The Web is an ideal library of source information for learners.

Preparing a class

The key limitation in using online materials is often the availability of Internet access in your classroom. There are obviously several different possibilities, such as:

> everyone can access online resources;
> only a single computer is available to access online resources.

It may seem a blessing for all your learners to have access, but the danger is that you will structure all the activities around the individual and the possibilities of small-group or whole-class exercises will be lost. Do not allow the provision of Internet access to dictate how you plan your learning objectives and methods. Make the situation fit your needs. Make sure that you use resources that fit your learning objectives and support your learners' needs. You might want to suggest that the individual or group print out all the relevant information and analyse them elsewhere. Computer rooms are not always the best places if you need space to discuss or lay out materials.

A single access point can appear very limiting, but there is no particular reason why everyone should undertake the same tasks at the same time. Develop a schedule to allow individuals or small groups to work on the online aspects while everyone else undertakes other activities. If you want to involve the whole group then use a data protector, so that everyone can see the screen.

It can often be too easy to see online resources in the context of the individual and miss the opportunities of small-group or whole-class approaches. Consider what you want to achieve and plan accordingly. There are substantial benefits in including activities for individuals, pairs, small groups and the whole class. It is good practice to vary your methods and offer learners a choice of methods.

For many learners, using online resources will be a new experience, so you need to brief them to ensure they will gain maximum benefit. There is a danger that they will not understand the point of going online unless this is clearly stated. An extra benefit of using online resources is that as each individual or group of learners locates new sites, you gain more materials or alternatives for the next group of learners.

Between sessions

A high proportion of households have access to the Internet, and public access through libraries, UK Online centres and other locations is widespread. It is likely that if you succeed in motivating your learners they will continue with the activities on their own between sessions. This offers the possibility of supporting learning by providing additional exercises. The obvious danger is that some people will not have Internet access nor have extra time available between sessions. You need to make sure they are not placed at a disadvantage. This is perhaps best achieved by suggesting only added-value actions between sessions while concentrating on the core curriculum in the formal meetings. Learners will usually have individual interests, so home activities can be focused on these.

If people do have Internet access then it is often beneficial to encourage email communication between them. So it is useful to ask the group if they would like to share email addresses in order to communicate between sessions. Again, the possibilities of small groups working together are obvious, but once again there is the risk of excluding some learners.

Online communication often reveals three broad categories of learner:

> *Activists* – who contribute a great deal – read everything that is sent and send their own emails in response;
> *Lurkers* – who read everything but rarely send their own messages;
> *Non-participants* – who rarely read or send messages.

7

Basically, the mere sharing of email addresses is no guarantee that people will communicate.

Summary

The main points of this section are:

> Learning is an active process.

> A constructivist approach is suitable for e-learning.

> The use of online resources is often engaging and motivating.

You need to:

> build on the benefits of e-learning;

> use online resources purposefully;

> decide on your role as a tutor and explain it to your learners;

> use Internet access flexibly and creatively;

> use individual, pair, small-group and whole-class approaches;

> provide activities for learners able to access the Internet between sessions;

> encourage email communication;

> avoid placing learners without access to the Internet at a disadvantage.

Photo: Nick Hayes. Using an interactive whiteboard in the classroom. Photo taken in the Brasshouse Language Centre in Birmingham.

3

Learning with online resources

Objectives

In all forms of learning the key defining factor is the learning objective that you are seeking to achieve. Using online resources does not change this. Learning objectives can be used to support a wide range of aims, such as:

> *Knowledge* – you may simply want your learners to gain an understanding of a topic, so the Web becomes a type of library in which they can seek information. However, you would rarely suggest that learners visit a library to locate content unless you were certain that it was present or that you had offered a range of alternatives. You might provide a list of titles or authors to narrow down and direct the search. In a similar way, using the Web you would have checked out sites or offered a range of search terms that would focus the exercise.

> *Discussion* – often you will want to encourage discussion, so rather than an individual activity you will ask a group of learners to locate information and come to conclusions about it. The Web is a very useful resource for facilitating discussion on almost every topic (e.g. news, science, history, geography).

> *Individual exercises* – you may want to use the online resource as a stimulus for an exercise such as creative writing, reading different types of material (e.g. news compared to government) or analysis of numerical information (e.g. weather, economics or savings).

> *Problem solving* – an individual or group activity could be to solve a particular problem with the assistance of a range of previously located websites.

> *Skills* – often you will be aiming to improve individual learning skills or the ability to learn in collaboration/co-operation with others. The Web provides a wealth of opportunities for activities which will help learners to develop their learning skills, such as:

  * note taking,
  * analysis,
  * working with others,
  * judging the quality and appropriateness of content.

> *Inspiration* – the Web can be used to provide ideas, instructions and alternative approaches to inspire learners on creative courses such as arts, crafts, dressmaking, embroidery, cross-stitch or many other forms of creative design.

> *Embedding* – it is often possible to embed learning about one subject within another. The obvious link in online activity is to include the development of information and communication skills within learning about other subjects online. Learners have the opportunity to develop skills such as searching, navigating, downloading and printing content.

Of course, these activities could make up an entire session, but more likely they will need to be integrated with more conventional approaches. This is a significant advantage in that you can vary the methods, contents and approaches for individuals so that you are more likely to meet their preferred learning styles.

All these suggestions are based on using the Web as a general educational resource. However, there are also many organisations that produce distinct learning content. These have a variety of names and come from many different sources. The Learning and Skills Council's National Learning Network (NLN) has produced approximately 1,000 hours of learning material for organisations that receive funding from them. Such materials are called learning objects and are discrete pieces of learning materials intended to provide chunks of learning in a range of subjects. In order to employ these resources effectively you need to plan your sessions so that they are fully integrated into your learning objectives.

Example

One NLN learning object provides a simulation to enable learners to combine different flowers into a range of displays. This has the advantage that learners can try many different combinations and permutations without the expense of buying flowers. In the classroom you might ask learners to plan their displays with the learning objective and then, in the next session, use real flowers to create the displays.

An alternative use of this learning object might be during an open day when you are trying to encourage people to return to learning. The flower arranging could be used as a fun demonstration of the possibilities of computers or later as a means of practising mouse skills such as dragging and dropping.

Your purpose determines the use of the resource, e.g. encouraging the return to learning, practising mouse and IT skills, and so on.

If you are planning to integrate online learning into your classes, you need to take the characteristics of online resources into consideration. These are very likely to influence the learning process because they are very different from 'traditional' media such as books or overhead projector slides. Below are some factors you might want to consider when preparing a class with online resources.

Hypertext/Hypermedia

The nature of online information is different from a paper publication in that it is based on hypertext/hypermedia. That is, a page of information is linked to other related chunks of information, whereas a paper publication follows a linear structure. The links can be from anything that appears on the page, such as a word, phrase, picture or

area. The normal convention of the Web is to underline words that link to other information and to change the shape of the mouse pointer to indicate when it is over a link. Learners are able to move between chunks of information by clicking with their mouse. The common problem is that it is very easy for learners to become unsure of where they are and how to return to their starting point. Tutors are frequently asked, 'How do I get back?' Figure 2 illustrates a page from 'Money matters to me' which has many different hyperlinks. The blue underlined text is a list of links to other sections, and you can also notice that the pointer has changed shape to become a hand. There are other links on this page; they can be revealed by placing the pointer over the down arrows.

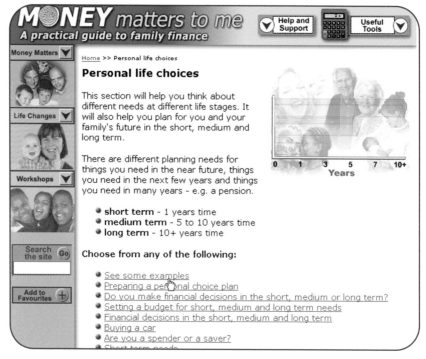

Figure 2 **Many links www.moneymatterstome.co.uk**
Note the pointer is now a hand selecting the first link in the list.

Navigation

A hypertext environment is rich and motivating but also potentially confusing. However, website designers have developed ways of helping you retrace your routes or understand the structure of the site. Towards the top of Figure 2 you should be able to locate another piece of blue underlined text (**Home**) indicating another link, in this case showing you the route you have taken. If you click on 'Home' you return to your starting place, in this case the homepage of the site. This feature is not always included; it is called a breadcrumb trail. When it is included, it is a very useful tool for moving around a site.

An alternative approach to navigation is to use the 'Forward' and 'Back' buttons on the browser that you use to move around the Web. Figure 3 shows Microsoft Internet Explorer. In the top left-hand corner are two buttons – 'Back' and 'Forward'. By clicking on these buttons you retrace your steps.

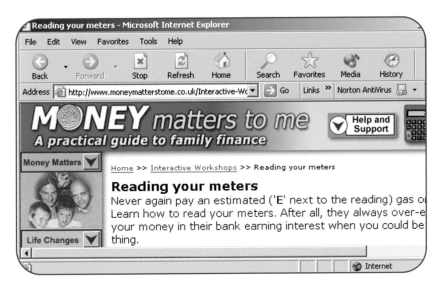

Figure 3 **Internet Explorer**

Many websites also give a site map to give users an overview of the whole online resource. A site map allows you to jump directly to any part of the site. Figure 4 illustrates the site map for 'Money matters to me'.

Website designers sometimes offer additional help to make it easier to move around the site without getting confused, and to retrace your steps, by adding buttons such as 'Top', 'Home' and 'Back' (Figure 5). These are often positioned at the top and bottom of each page. By clicking on them you can control your movements. These are very useful when the page of information is so long that as you scroll down you lose sight of the titles. They also have the additional benefit of making movements faster.

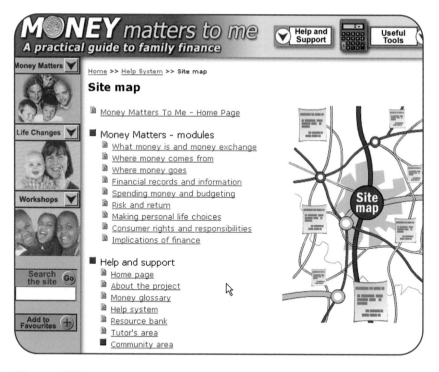

Figure 4 **Site map**

For effective Web browsing the skills of moving around and retracing your steps are essential, so in the early stages of using online resources it is appropriate to build in exercises to help learners to develop their skills.

Example

Probably the best way of developing navigation skills is to *use* the Web to find some information after, a brief introduction explaining various aids to navigation, such as:

> breadcrumb trails,
> browser 'Forward' and 'Back' buttons,
> site navigation buttons,
> site maps.

You could use a video projector and demonstrate to the whole group what these various aids do and then ask them to practise using them while carrying out a task. It is important to show new users the effects of scrolling down a page, losing sight of the top headings and then jumping into the middle of another page. Even the most experienced user can become confused when that happens.

Practice is important, so continue to reinforce the concepts.

Photo: Nick Hayes. Using Internet Resources in the classroom. Photo taken in the Brasshouse Language Centre in Birmingham.

Searching

Navigating around an individual website or across the whole Web is a critical skill, but it is equally important to be able to find the information you are seeking. Many learning activities are based on asking learners to search the Web to locate information (e.g. a quiz, researching a topic and undertaking a task). Large websites often provide search facilities to help you locate information on the site. Figure 5 shows the results of a site search. The search was undertaken by entering the word 'housing' into the search window and clicking on the 'Go' button. The result was a list of possible links to housing, which can then be accessed by a click.

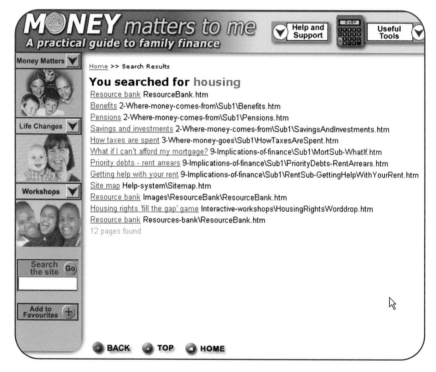

Figure 5 **Site search engine**

To search the whole of the Web rather than merely an individual site you must use a search engine. This is a program or system that searches web pages for specified keywords and returns a list of the documents where the keywords were found. Well known and easily accessible search engines include Google, Alta Vista and Excite.

The number of pages that a search engine can examine is prodigious – well over eight billion are searched by Google as of November 2004.

There are now three main types of search engine:

> *Individual* – an engine with its own database;
> *Meta* – an engine which searches through several databases of individual engines;
> *Directory* – essentially a list of sites identified by the staff of the engine under a variety of popular subjects (e.g. shopping).

Directories are often provided as part of individual and meta search engines.

The many different search engines can produce very different results.

Example

A search for "learning resources" on **www.google.co.uk** and **www.dogpile.com** got these results:

Google – 2,040,000 hits
Dogpile – 81 hits

Searching the Web is an essential skill for using online resources and it is appropriate to build in exercises to help learners to develop their skills.

Searching practice needs to cover:

> the different types of search engine;
> searching methods
>> key words
>> using inverted commas
>> using + and –
>> boolean (And, Or, Not)

The whole process of searching for information about a topic can be used to illustrate its characteristics.

The quality of online resources

Anyone can develop a website and publish their own information to the world. This is a wonderful development but also a major issue for people using the Web as a learning resource, since the immediate questions arise: What is the quality of the content? Is the material accurate, or simply the opinions of one particular individual? There is no single factor that enables one to determine the quality of content, but a range of issues that need to be considered:

> Who owns the site? (Are they likely to know about the subject of the site?)
> When was the site last updated? (Very important in a dynamic area where issues change daily.)
> Does the content of the site agree with other sources of information?
> How is the site linked to or from others?

Judging the quality of information on the Web is an important skill when using online resources, so it is appropriate to build in exercises to help learners to develop their expertise in this area.

Example

Ask learners to locate information on a particular topic and list the sites in order of quality.

This would form the basis for a class discussion around what people judge as quality content.

Bookmarking

Once you have located a useful website it is important to use the bookmarking features of the browser (e.g. 'Favorites' in Internet Explorer) to make sure you can find it again. Within a short period of using the Web with learners you will gather a large resource of sites for different purposes.

Access

The Web is not universally designed for visually impaired learners. However, many sites specifically designed for education have tried to provide accessible content. To learn more about accessibility visit:

> **bobby.watchfire.com/bobby/html/en/index.jsp** – a free tool to assess the accessibility of Web pages;

> **www.techdis.ac.uk** – information for disabled education staff and learners with disabilities;

> **www.w3.org/WAI** – a Web accessibility initiative.

Accessibility is not limited to websites, but is also concerned with the hardware and systems used for searching the Web. The Microsoft Windows operating system provides many straightforward ways of improving access. These are available from the 'Control Panel', 'Accessibility Options'. Figure 6 shows the Accessibility Options display in Windows XP.

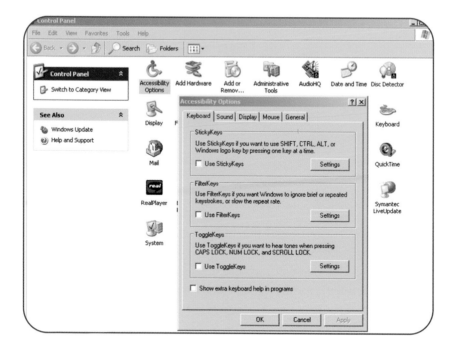

Figure 6 **Accessibility Options display**

Windows Accessibility Options enable you to make changes to the keyboard, mouse, sound, and display. Explore what they provide and you will in many cases be able to remove some of the barriers which your learners encounter in using a computer.

Copyright

Everything published on the Web is governed by copyright. You should assume that you need the permission of the owners to use the material in any way other than simply visiting the site and reading the information. In many cases this is all that you want to do, so you are not limited, but in other cases you will wish to go further. Many sites will give an explanation of how the site works and copyright details. Seek out the site's copyright guidance and check what you need to do.

Example

'Money matters to me' – copyright question and answer

'Can I use downloaded resources for my own educational materials?'

'Yes, we want you to use this site as a resource within educational situations, so feel free to download the downloadable version of this site and then either use "as is" or cut and paste sections across to your own materials. All we would ask is that wherever possible and practical you credit the source (this resource) and that you do not use any materials for commercial purposes at any time. Click here to go to the downloads section now.'

Choosing the right e-learning materials for your learners

There are increasing amounts of online and e-learning content available, so it is important to select the most appropriate and useful material. At the NLN showcase conference in Coventry in 2003 a group of practitioners considered the issues of making such choices, and the content of this section is based on their efforts. The workshop considered learning content that was both free and for sale, information and interactive learning packages, and online and stand-alone content.

Learning

There are three fundamental issues associated with learning to consider when assessing content:

> What learning styles does it employ? (Meaning 'Which learners will it benefit?')

> What learning skills are needed to use the content effectively?

> What computer skills are required to make the best use of the content?

Foundation principles

There are three foundation principles that probably apply to all learning materials of all types:

> The content should be 'age appropriate'. That is suitable for adult learners. This is significant when a large volume of online content is aimed at schoolchildren rather than adults.
> The content should reflect cultural diversity.
> The content should avoid gender stereotyping.

General principles

There are seven general principles to consider, implicit in the following questions:

> Who are your learners? What are their needs? Is the content appropriate to them?
> How flexible is the content? Can you adapt it to meet your needs?
> How is the content assessed?
> How is the learning designed?
> What learner support is assumed in the design or provided by the vendor?
> What learning strategy is assumed within the design of the content?
> How is the material presented? What is the quality of the design?

Evaluation

There are four things to consider in evaluating content:

> Has the content been reviewed? Can you locate a published review?
> Can you get an e-learning specialist to review content?
> It is important to involve your learners in evaluating content.
> How easy is the content to install, and does it require particular technical skills to use?

Evaluation methods

Four evaluation methods are:

> Interview learners who have used the material.

> Bring together a focus group of learners and/or tutors to evaluate the content.

> Use a questionnaire to find out the opinions of a large group of learners or tutors.

> Observe learners using the content.

Figure 7 is a checklist of the issues that you might want to consider in assessing the usefulness and appropriateness of e-learning materials.

☐ Learner-centredness: Can learners control the sequence and pace of learning?

☐ Learner-friendliness: Is the content clear and easy to use?

☐ Good use of technology: Are multimedia and hypertext used to motivate and support the learner and to enrich the learning process?

☐ Adaptability: Can the content be adapted to different learners and their needs?

☐ Motivation: Is the content motivating and engaging?

☐ Self-assessment: does the resource support the self-assessment of learners?

☐ Learning value: Does the e-resource have clear advantages over books?

☐ Compatibility: Is the content compatible with other systems and resources?

☐ Are help and support available?

☐ Usability: Is the resource easy to use with existing equipment?

☐ Archiving: Can learners archive/save their work and return to the same point later?

☐ Evaluation: How can tutors access what learners have done?

☐ Collaborative: Does the resource support collaborative learning, and is it interactive?

☐ Learning skills: What ICT and learning skills do learners need to use the resource?

Figure 7 **Checklist for analysing e-learning content**

Summary

The main points of this section are:

> Learning objectives are the key defining factor for choosing learning resources.

> Online resources can support a wide range of learning objectives.

> Your purpose determines the use of the resource.

> Online information is based on hypertext.

> Navigation skills for online resources are essential.

> Searching and finding information on the Web are essential skills.

> It is important to be able to judge the quality of online resources for using them in a learning context.

> You need to check your equipment and software against accessibility options.

> Everything published on the Web is governed by copyright.

> It is important to select e-learning content that is appropriate for your learners and their needs.

4

Blended learning

Introduction

Blended learning is the integration of conventional approaches with e-learning to gain the benefits of both. Figure 8 shows an interactive exercise from the 'Money matters to me' resource which is intended to help people learn about budgeting. A similar exercise could be done with paper and pencil in the classroom. The benefit of using an online resource is that you can do the exercise many times, allowing you to experiment with different options – print out the final budget so everyone can share the outcome, use a data projector so that the whole group can share the experience and add a motivational experience to the exercise by going online. You could use the online exercise as a starting point to a detailed learning process about budgettingbudgeting, with the next steps including learners calculating their own expenditure for a typical week. Fieldwork could be included in that the group could visit a supermarket together to consider purchasing options. There are many integration possibilities.

What is important is to consider what your objectives are for the session and how the different aspects could best be blended together.

Example

If your objectives included helping the group learn how to use the Web so that they could learn how to shop online, then you have an extra reason for using the online exercise.

Photo: Nick Hayes. Example showing blended learning at Age Concern Café, Chislehurst.

There are many other resources available on the Web that you could integrate into your courses. The **www.aclearn.net** site (Figure 9) has a resource exchange that is well worth visiting to locate e-learning materials for your programmes.

Using online resources

There are many online resources that you can use as part of a course of study. They can be employed for individuals, small groups and the whole class, depending on what you are seeking to achieve. Or you might want to structure a whole session or course around a single site. Money matters to me is a resource that could form the basis of an entire course. There are other sites that also offer considerable resources. Below are some examples of online resources that are useful for teaching and learning. (Do bear in mind that these are just examples; it might be worth exploring the Internet yourself to find resources that are useful for your subjects.)

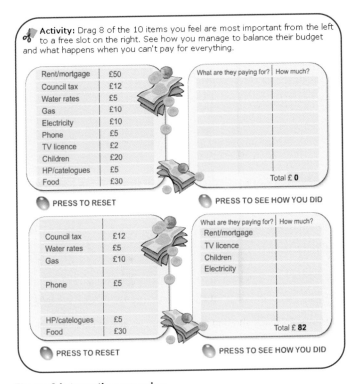

Figure 8 **Interactive exercise**

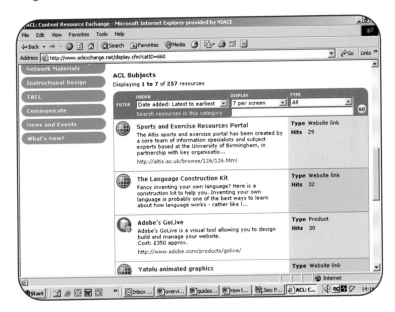

Figure 9 **The www.aclearn.net resource exchange**

Single sites

These are two examples of websites that you might want to structure a whole session or course around.

Example

National Gallery

www.nationalgallery.org.uk/education/visits/resources.htm

The National Gallery offers significant resources for educators, primarily aimed at schools, but potentially very useful in adult education. The site includes:

> Detailed notes for teachers about particular paintings and suggestions for learning activities for primary schools (adaptable for an adult group). You could build a whole programme around these resources

> Facilities for searching and browsing the whole collection

> Facilities for enlarging pictures online

> Biographies of several leading artists

The resources within the National Gallery could provide the basis of a whole course or many online exercises and activities.

Example

BBC Learning

www.bbc.co.uk/learning/

A considerable resource to help learning in a wide range of subjects (e.g. health, study skills, geography, history). There are several online courses, as well as information and other forms of content.

Languages

The Web consists predominantly of many thousands of English-language sites, but many other languages are available to provide resources for people studying them or for people seeking to keep in touch with developments in their country of original. A simple search using the word 'French' resulted in:

> One site advertising French language resources
> Two sites with French-to-English and English-to-French dictionaries
> One site of a French language association
> One site of a French tourist office
> Three French-language sites

This simple search revealed several possibilities:

> The French-language sites could provide opportunities to read French – if they are news sites, then the possibility of considering a comparison of how a story was reported in France and the UK.
> The tourist information site offers possibilities of obtaining information about France, focusing an exercise around planning a holiday and involving writing letters to French hotels to book accommodation. This gives the opportunity of customising language activities.
> Dictionary sites provide access to these valuable resources for the whole class.

For you the Web is an inspiration to help you plan your classes. You could, for example, use the content of the French news sites in the form of printouts rather than online. The choice is yours.

Example

Tate Modern Gallery

www.tate.org.uk/home/french.htm

Many public sites offer the opportunity to view their contents in several languages. The Tate Modern provides the facility to view the contents in:

> English

> French

> Spanish

> German

> Italian

> Japanese

This offers a wealth of possibilities for language classes. The site also offers a free online level 1 course, 'Introducing Learners to Art'.

Simulations

Many websites provide access to online simulations. These include:

> science experiments

> demonstrations of products

> virtual tours

Example

Virtual Tour

www.number-10.gov.uk/output/page41.asp

The website linked to 10 Downing Street offers the opportunity of taking a virtual tour of the building. This allows you to explore the different rooms and consider their history, and provides information about government structures. This could form the basis of many different sessions, such as:

> Citizenship

> History

> ICT – navigation

discussion – use a data projector to provide a whole class resource

Example

Multimedia Presentations
www.sciencemuseum.org.uk/nakedscience

Many sites offer access to multimedia presentations. The Science Museum website 'naked science' section offers the opportunity to watch and listen to a discussion about science topics.

Example

The 'Money matters to me' site **www.moneymatterstome.co.uk** offers you a series of interactive workshops, including a simulation of a cash machine.

Resources

Many sites offer resources in a variety of forms. The example below offers a vast collection of images which you can use for educational purposes.

Example

Astronomy/Space Flight
www.nasa.gov/home/index.html

This example is based on the NASA website which offers resources for educators. It provides content for children of different ages as well as for post-secondary and informal learners. There is a vast range of material and you should explore the site to identify the possibilities, but amongst the resources is the NASA Image Exchange (NIX), which offers access to a collection of 300,000 images linked to space exploration and related subjects. The copyright declaration on the site allows the free use of these images for educational purposes.

This large collection could provide material for a variety of purposes, such as:

> Visual aids for presentations

> Resources for practising desktop publishing

> Project work illustrations

> Worksheet illustrations

Example

Construction/Architecture
www.greatbuildings.com

This example shows architecture around the world, including photographs of buildings, 3-D models, architectural drawings, commentaries and bibliographies. This could provide material for:

> Photographic images for presentations or worksheets

> Resources for discussing building plans

Example

Building Regulations: Office of the Deputy Prime Minister
www.odpm.gov.uk/stellent/groups/odpm_buildreg/documents/
sectionhomepage/odpm_buildreg_page.hcsp

This example gives information about building regulations in the UK. This resource can be used:

> As a resource for finding information on building regulations

> As a resource for worksheets

> As a resource for project work

Example

Science
www.ingenious.org.uk

This website draws on the resources of the National Museum for Science and Industry and brings together images and viewpoints to create insights into science and culture. Subjects and topics put these images in context and give historical and cultural insights on current issues in science, technology and medicine. This might be useful for:

> Photographic images

> Material for individual student projects

> A resource for webquests

Example

Mathematics

www.mathsnet.net

This is an independent educational website providing free mathematics resources. It includes discussion forums, puzzles and reviews of calculators, software and books. This might be useful for the:

> Preparation of classes

> Use of interactive exercises for teaching mathematics

Example

Electronics

www.circuit-fantasia.com

This website is an interactive multimedia product consisting of tutorials, collections of circuits, basic principles and heuristic tools. This might be useful:

> As a resource to explain electric circuits

> As a resource for learners to explore independently

Example

Arts and Humanities

www.aldaily.com

An example of a weblog, providing links to newspaper and journal articles, book reviews and extracts, essays and hundreds of websites of newspapers, periodicals, TV and radio stations, individuals and organisations.

This might be useful for:

> Preparation of discussions on philosophy, literature, language, culture, history, music or art

> Current Affairs, Media Studies and International Relations

> A resource for webquests

The Adult and Community Learning site (**www.aclearn.net**) offers a resource exchange.

Tools and aids

There are many different ways in which online resources can be useful. Many of them are relatively small but can be very helpful. Some examples are:

> *Exchange-rate calculators* – there are a range of sites providing currency conversion calculators and many more giving the current rates.

> *Automatic translation* – on the AltaVista search engine site an automated translation service is provided which will translate text from one language to another, or you can select a webpage to be translated – **babel.altavista.com/translate.dyn**

> *Maps* – there are several excellent map sites on the Web. The Ordnance Survey offers the 'Get A Map' service on their site, but do read the conditions for use –
www.ordnancesurvey.co.uk/oswebsite
Other map sites include:
> Multilimap **www.multimap.com**
> Mappy **www.mappy.com**

> *Weather* – the Meteorological Office site (**www.meto.gov.uk**) gives national and international weather forecasts. However, the site is rich in content and has a section for teachers, even though it is essentially aimed at children. There are many useful resources which you could adapt for adults, and a teacher training centre aimed at helping teachers improve their skills and understanding about the climate.

> *Financial aids* – The 'Money matters to me' site (**www.moneymatterstome.co.uk/**) offers a range of tools and interactive workshops that will assist a financial education programme such as:
> various calculators (e.g. loan, mortgage and debt repayment)

> reading meters (e.g. electricity)
> simulation of a cash machine

> *Images* – several search engines allow you to search for images relating to a particular topic on the Web, e.g. **www.google.co.uk**

> *Video* – the World Bank site (**info.worldbank.org/etools/bspan/Top10.asp**) offers access to a range of online video that discusses key issues

> *Creation tools* – Hot Potatoes (**www.halfbakedsoftware.com**) is an authoring tool which is free if you are working in state-funded education and make your products freely available – as always, do read the conditions for use.

> There are many products made using Hot Potatoes that you may find useful, such as **www.ucl.ac.uk/learningtechnology/information/technology/hotpot** and **ferl.becta.org.uk**; and try an online search to locate more.

> *Resources* – the ELDIS site provides many links to educational resources **www.eldis.org/education/toolsresources.htm**

Worksheets

ICT provides many tools to help you design worksheets. For example, independently of any online learning resources, applications such as Microsoft Word and Microsoft Publisher are very useful in creating worksheets. There are two main uses of online content when designing worksheets:

> to provide direct content (e.g. insert image);
> to direct learners to sites so that additional information can be gained, or to enhance the learning process.

Creation

Worksheets can take a variety of forms but must provide a clear statement of what the learner will gain from undertaking the activities described within the worksheet.

> ## Example
>
> After undertaking these activities you will be able to:
>
> _____

> Worksheets are often helpful in areas of the curriculum that learners find difficult.

> Each worksheet should provide learners with a systematic, logical step-by-step explanation, with questions to reflect on and self-study activities.

> The presentation should be clear, using plain English and illustrations.

Websites

Integrating visits to websites into worksheets is potentially a very powerful aid to learning. You can add considerable value by using information from the Web. However, it is vital to realise that the Web is a dynamic resource which is continually changing. This makes checking website content and addresses a critical part of preparing a new course.

Worksheets are just one way of preparing a class. Do bear in mind that a variety of teaching and learning methods is most likely to be motivating and supportive for learners.

Quizzes

Quizzes can be used in almost every subject and context. They are fun and engaging, and can be a useful way to learn. They can provide a means of assessment, both initial, to help you plan the programme, and summative. The online aspect can add value in several ways:

> Online resources can help people answer the questions, so encouraging learners to seek out information.

> Communications technology can allow a quiz to be conducted at a distance. Two or more teams can take part who would normally be unable to meet because of distance or other factors.

> Online resources can help devise questions, and a useful variation on a standard quiz is to ask the learners to develop the questions.

> Searching skills can be practised and the ability to judge the quality of online information can be developed.

Example 1

Astronomy – The Solar System

This could be used for a range of objectives, such as:

> encouraging collaboration;

> locating information for the quiz to set the questions or to provide answers;

> individual initial assessment, or to open a discussion about what people hoped to gain from a course;

> encouraging the development of search techniques.

1 How many planets are there in the solar system?

2 How far from the sun is the earth?

3 Which is the red planet?

4 Ganymede is a moon circling which planet?

5 When was Pluto discovered?

6 Which planet has rings?

7 What planet is nearest to the sun?

8 When did men first land on the moon?

9 Who was the first man to travel in space?

10 Deimos is a moon of which planet?

Example 2

Citizenship

This could be used for a range of objectives, such as:

> discussion topics for group activities;

> helping people to understand the structure of the British government;

> an individual initial assessment or to open a discussion about what people hoped to gain from a course;

> encouraging the development of search techniques.

1 How old must you be:

(a) to vote?

(b) to get married?

(c) to drive a car?

2 Who is the Secretary of State for Education?

3 Which tax was an emergency wartime measure?

4 How many countries are members of the European Union?

5 In which capital city are the main offices of the European Union?

6 The International Court of Justice meets in what European city?

7 The United Nations was formed after which world war?

8 Who are five permanent members of the UN Security Council?

Webquests

Webquests are a very flexible and powerful way to help learning. They can be used with individuals or small groups, depending on the objectives you are seeking to achieve. A webquest is often presented to learners in the form of:

1 Scenario,
2 Task,
3 Recommended resources.

The scenario provides the background to the quest and resembles the types of brief that are provided during a role-playing exercise: it is perfectly possible to give a webquest a large element of role-play if that contributes to the objective. If you were seeking to develop collaborative skills you might well develop a quest based around a group activity where each member of the group took on distinct roles (e.g. co-ordinator, scribe, manager, etc.). Alternatively, if you were attempting to help learners understand other perspectives you might ask individuals to undertake the tasks of a police officer, politician, or managing director of a multinational company.

The tasks are the details of the aims or objectives you would like the questers to achieve during the webquest. These could be presented as a list of questions to be answered or objectives to be met. You can define small or large quests so that you may provide a single task or a range of interlocking issues to solve. Again, it depends on what you are seeking to achieve.

The final section is a list of online resources which provide all the information required to fulfil the webquest. The overall objective is not to simply locate useful information but rather to analyse and use the information to meet a challenge, in this case the tasks defined by the quest.

Photo: Nick Hayes. Example of collaborative learning, taken in the
Brasshouse Centre, Birmingham.

The length of a webquest can be short (say, 20 minutes) or long
(covering many weeks). It is sometimes important to indicate to the
learners what the overall time scale is.

The National Learning Network Adult and Community learning
website, AClearn (**www.aclearn.net**), has help and support for tutors
wanting to use webquests in the form of a toolkit. On 'Money matters
to me' you can find a number of webquests designed for working
with the site.

Example 1

This example is aimed at a team of ICT tutors and aims to assist their professional development in relation to changes to ICT qualifications, and in particular ICT as a Skill for Life.

Webquest: ICT Skill for Life

Scenario: You have been asked by your manager to consider the implications of the new ICT Skill for Life standard.

Task: Your tasks are to:

> Obtain copies of the ICT Skills for Life standard.

> Consider how it relates to existing qualifications such as New CLAIT and CLAIT Plus and identify any related developments (e.g. National Occupational Standards and Learning and Skills Council ITQ qualification).

> Discuss what actions, if any, your organisation should take.

> Write a short report, with recommendations, for your manager.

Recommended resources: To undertake this task you might want to take a look at the following resources:

> ICT Skills for Life standard
   www.qca.org.uk/qualifications/types/2791.html
> ICT Users
   www.e-skills.com/cgi-bin/wms.pl/136
> e-passport
   www.e-skills.com/cgi-bin/wms.pl/220
> OCR awarding body for New CLAIT and CLAIT Plus
   www.ocr.org.uk
> Standards Unit – Professional development
   www.successforall.gov.uk

Example 2

This example is aimed at learners who want to gain an understanding of government.

Webquest: **Citizenship**

Scenario: Your 18th birthday is approaching and you will have the opportunity to vote in a national election for the first time. You would like to improve your understanding of parliament and government structures so that you can make a well-informed decision about who to vote for.

Task: Your tasks are to:

> investigate the different roles of the House of Commons and the House of Lords;

> identify how Parliament works;

> identify your Member of Parliament;

> identify the role of the European Parliament.

Recommended resources:

> House of Commons and House of Lords
  www.parliament.uk

> Lists of Members of Parliament
  www.parliament.uk/directories/hciolists/alms.cfm

> European Parliament
  www.europarl.eu.int/home/default_en.htm

Example 3

This example is aimed at learners returning to employment after a break.

Webquest: **Financial education**

Scenario: You are about to return to work after a break while you have been looking after your children and family. You need to know what you will pay in Income Tax and National Insurance contributions.

Task: Your tasks are to identify:

> what tax allowance you will receive;

> the tax rates that currently apply;

> the amount you can earn without paying National Insurance;

> the amount of National Insurance you need to pay;

> any schemes that might benefit you;

> how self-assessment affects you.

Recommended resources:

> Returning to work
  www.moneymatterstome.co.uk/ReturningToWork.htm

> Income tax
  www.moneymatterstome.co.uk/3-Where-money-goes/Sub1/IncomeTax.htm

> National Insurance
  www.moneymatterstome.co.uk/3-Where-money-goes/Sub1/NationalInsurance.htm

> The Inland Revenue
  www.inlandrevenue.gov.uk

Figure 10 illustrates one of the resource pages which offers information required for the webquest.

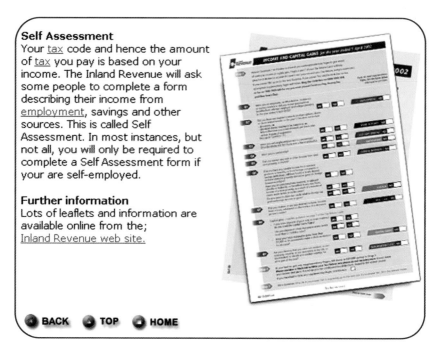

Self Assessment
Your tax code and hence the amount of tax you pay is based on your income. The Inland Revenue will ask some people to complete a form describing their income from employment, savings and other sources. This is called Self Assessment. In most instances, but not all, you will only be required to complete a Self Assessment form if your are self-employed.

Further information
Lots of leaflets and information are available online from the;
Inland Revenue web site.

BACK   TOP   HOME

Figure 10 **Self Assessment**

Investigations

Investigations are more open-ended than a webquest and ask learners individually or in small groups to research a topic. While a webquest puts the emphasis on analysing the information on sites which are suggested to them, an investigation requires learners to identify suitable sources of information as well as to analyse the content. It requires:

> good search skills;
> judgement of the quality of the information;
> analysis of the information.

It is important to identify specific learning objectives for the investigation. The risk is that if it is too general learners will not be clear about why they are undertaking the task. Inspection reports have sometimes commented that learners are not sure why they are using the Internet. Good practice would be to:

> identify specific learning objectives;
> brief the learners so they are clear about the task;
> integrate the investigation into the course.

Creating content

Creating materials in any form is often a very motivating and interesting experience, so offering learners the opportunity to be creative in developing materials that will be published online is well worth considering. There are several readily available tools which might usefully be employed, such as:

> Hot Potatoes,
> Microsoft FrontPage – for creating webpages,
> Microsoft PowerPoint,
> CourseGenie,
> Paint Shop Pro,
> Adobe Photoshop,
> Dreamweaver XP,
> Kallidus Authorising Tool,
> Seminar,
> Paintshop Pro,
> Viewlet Builder 4 Professional.

A digital camera can also play an important role in allowing learners to illustrate their work. If you can link a camera with editing software it is a very powerful combination. Learner-created content can often serve as examples for other groups or a focus for exercises, assignments and projects.

Creating content can be used in almost all areas of the curriculum such as:

> ESOL – focus for a project (e.g. planning a journey);
> local history – preparing a presentation on a local area;
> science – explaining a topic (e.g. land and sea breezes);
> creative writing;
> arts and crafts.

Almost any learning group will benefit from their work being made available to a wider audience. In adult education, the open day or other form of presentation of work produced by learners have been employed for many years to motivate people to return to learning and to give existing groups and individuals an exciting objective. For more on creating content and on the use of digital cameras see e-guidelines 2, *Digital Cameras in Teaching and Learning*, by Phil Hardcastle, and e-guidelines 3, *Developing Your Own e-learning Materials*, by Shubhanna Hussain (both published by NIACE, 2004).

Communication

The use of communication technologies is a factor to consider when you are blending online resources into your learning programmes. The most common method is probably email, which can be very effective in allowing learners to continue to discuss their ideas and experiences between face-to-face sessions. It also offers the possibility of making links with other groups considering the same or similar subjects who are too far away to meet. For language learners the possibilities of communicating and practising language skills are apparent.

The potential is obvious, but realising the possibilities is more difficult. Simply sharing email addresses is likely to be a hit-and-miss approach to effective communication. It needs to be done within a suitable context, such as a learning task to be undertaken. You will probably need to help start the process with some early messages to encourage people to join in with continuous monitoring to assist participation. It is important to stress also that a code of conduct needs to be established. This is often called netiquette, and a useful initial exercise is to ask the groups or groups to agree their own standards. Recent research has shown that good online communication conduct is important to the success of the discussion (Preece, 2004)

Integration

Blended learning is about the effective integration of online and e-learning resources with traditional methods. The photograph below demonstrates how learners are using interactive voting equipment. This is one example of how you can integrate traditional methods with e-learning.

Photo: Nick Hayes. Example of the use of voting equipment in the classroom, taken in Wolverhampton.

Summary

The main points of this section are:

> Blended learning is the integration of conventional approaches with e-learning.
> The Web can be a helpful resource for planning your lessons.
> You might want to structure a whole session or class around a single site, if appropriate.
> Online resources can give you useful tools and aids.
> Online resources can be helpful resources for creating worksheets.
> It is vital to check website content on a regular basis because the Web is dynamic and change occurs continuously.
> Online resources can be very valuable for preparing and conducting quizzes.
> Webquests are structured exercises that are very flexible and can be a powerful aid in learning.
> Investigations are powerful processes, requiring learners to identify suitable sources of information, and they enhance analytic skills.
> Online tools that allow learners to create content can be very motivating.
> The use of communication technologies can support continuous learning outside the classroom.

5

Conclusion

There is no single best approach to using online learning content but some good practice ideas are:

> Actively involve your learners.

> Allow your learners to create their own knowledge while you support them.

> Base your exercises and activities on 'real-life' issues relevant to your learners.

> Employ a range of methods, including working in small groups, and encourage collaborative learning.

> Use simulators and multimedia to practise something that is intimidating (e.g. using a cash machine) or impractical to undertake in a classroom.

> Design the learning programme around your learners' needs and contexts.

> Integrate online material with more traditional methods – try to get the best from them.

> Make the learning fun and interesting.

> Use the Web in your own preparation.

> Encourage peer support.

> Share resources and exchange your experiences with your colleagues.

> Use the Internet for specific topics to demonstrate the richness of resources.

> Build your learners' confidence in using the Internet.

Further reading and resources

Books and papers

BBC and Becta (2003) *Using BBC online resources in your centre*, London: Becta and BBC.

Becta (2001) *Creating Online Learning Materials*, London: National Learning Network.

Clarke, A. (2001) *Designing Computer-based Learning Materials*, Aldershot: Gower.

Clarke, A. (2002) *Assessing the Quality of Open and Distance Learning Materials*, Leicester: NIACE.

Clarke, A. (2004) *e-learning Skills*, Basingstoke: Palgrave Macmillan.

Collis, B. (1996), *Tele-learning in a Digital World: Making Connections*, International Thomson Computer Press.

Collis, B., and Moonen, J. (2001) *Flexible Learning in a Digital World: Experiences and Expectations*, London: RoutledgeFalmer.

Hardcastle, P. (2004) *Digital Cameras in Teaching and Learning*, Leicester: NIACE.

Hussain, S. (2004) *Developing Your own e-Learning Materials: Applying user-centred design techniques to creating learning materials for adults*, Leicester: NIACE.

ICT Advice (2003) *Using Web-based Resources in Secondary Science*, London: Becta ICT Advice.

ICT Advice (2003) *Using Web-based Resources in Secondary History*, London: Becta ICT Advice.

Newman, D. (2003) *Embedding ILT into the Curriculum*, London: NLN, LSDA.

Preece, J. (2004) *Etiquette Online: From Nice to Necessary*, Communications of the ACM.

Salmon, G. (2002) *E-tivities: The Key to Active Online Learning*, London:RoutledgeFalmer.

Websites

The Web is a dynamic environment where sites change rapidly, so
you may find that these resources have altered since this guide was
written.

www.abilitynet.org.uk – advice on accessibility.
www.accessart.org.uk – art in museums and galleries.
www.aclearn.net – resources and information about the use of e-learning in
  Adult and Community Learning.
babel.altavista.com/translate.dyn – automated translation from one
  language to another.
www.bbc.co.uk/learning – BBC Learning Online resources, covering a
  wide range of subjects.
bobby.watchfire.com/bobby/html/en/index.jsp – a free tool to assess the
  accessibility of webpages.
www.channel4.com/learning – Channel 4's online learning resources.
www.classical-composers.org/cgi-bin/ccd.cgi – database of classical
  composers.
www.curriculumonline.gov.uk – Curriculum Online resources for schools.
www.dgray.com/index.htm – jigsaws galore.
www.digitalartsource.com/index2.shtml – digital art.
www.eldis.org/education/toolsresources.htm – online tools and resources
  for education.
www.enrichuk.net – link to online resources supported by the New
  Opportunities fund.
www.europarl.eu.int/home/default_en.htm – the European Parliament.
www.expertgardener.com/index2.asp – expert gardener.
www.ferl.org.uk – resources and information about how to use information
  and learning technology (ILT).
www.freepatternsonline.com – free cross-stitch and quilt patterns.
www.google.co.uk – search for pictures.
www.halfbakedsoftware.com – Hot Potatoes e-learning authoring tool.
www.helpisathand.gov.uk – resources for UK Online centres and
  community learning.
www.hmc.gov.uk – the Historical Manuscripts Commission site, which
  provides guides to family, local and house history.
www.iamdyslexia.com – ideas to help learners with dyslexia.
www.ictadvice.org.uk – advice on using ICT in learning for schools.
www.imagesofengland.org.uk – the English Heritage collection of
  photographs of listed buildings in England.
www.meto.gov.uk – the Meteorological Office site, rich in educational
  resources.

www.moneymatterstome.co.uk – free resources for adult financial education.

www.multimap.com – mapping resources.

www.nasa.gov/home/index.html – images and other resources linked to space travel and related topics.

www.nationalgallery.org.uk/education/visits/resources.htm – the National Gallery's educational resources.

www.nln.ac.uk/materials – a large collection of learning objects for post-16 organisations and tutors funded by the Learning and Skills Council.

www.number-10.gov.uk/output/page41.asp – a virtual tour of 10 Downing Street.

www.open2.net/home2/learning.html – an Open University and BBC partnership for learning resources.

www.ordnancesurvey.co.uk/oswebsite – the Ordnance Survey.

www.parliament.uk/explore_parliament/explore_parliament.cfm – education resources about parliament.

portal.unesco.org/education – UNESCO Education site.

www.sciencemuseum.org.uk/nakedscience – multimedia presentations on science topics.

www.streamingstories.org.uk – online stories.

www.tate.org.uk/home/french.htm – the Tate Gallery modern languages.

www.techdis.ac.uk – help for disabled learners and staff in using technology.

www.ucl.ac.uk/learningtechnology/information/technology/hotpot – examples of Hot Potatoes materials.

www.vts.rdn.ac.uk/teachers – free tutorials on using the Internet.

www1.worldbank.org/education – World Bank Education resources, covering many interesting subjects.

webquest.sdsu.edu/overview.htm – San Diego State University Webquest resources.

www.w3.org/WAI – a web accessibility initiative.

7
Glossary

Definitions that we suggest for terms used in this publication.

Active learning Learning that emphasises the learner's own initiative and activity. It assumes that learning is always an active process, in contrast with the traditional concept of teaching, where teachers deliver knowledge to learners.

Blended learning Integrating e-learning with conventional approaches to gain the benefits of using online resources in a face-to-face context.

Constructivism Constructivism (in the context of learning) is based on the assumption that learning is an active process and that learners create their own knowledge, based on their own individual experiences and contexts.

e-learning Learning in a way that uses information and communication technologies.

Hypermedia Extends the notion of hypertext to include links among any set of multimedia objects, including sound, video, and virtual reality. *See also* hypertext.

Hypertext : A text of information that is linked to other related chunks of information. Words, phrases or areas in a document that a reader can identify and select, and which cause another document to be retrieved and displayed. *See also* Hypermedia.

ICT Information and Communication Technologies.

ILT Information and Learning Technologies.

Link: Short for hyperlink. A word, picture or other area in a document that users can click on to move to another area in the document. *See also* hypertext.

Lurking A phenomenon that occurs frequently in discussion forums and message boards. It describes the behaviour of participants who read posted messages and observe the activity but who do not actively contribute by posting messages themselves.

Multimedia The integration of different presentation formats, e.g. video, text, graphics, sound, audio, etc. Multimedia can have a positive effect on learning because it can stimulate different senses and different ways of processing information.

Online learning Learning with the help of ICT and ILT that requires a connection to the Internet.

Weblog (often shortened to blog) A personal or non-commercial website that uses a dated diary or log format updated very frequently with new information or links about a particular range of subjects. The information can be written by the site-owner, extracted from websites or other sources, or contributed by users.